THE PIERIAN

Volume I
2023

The Pierian is a journal of poetry
published annually

EDITORS:　　Max Roland Ekstrom

Keeley Schell

Order issues and read the latest poetry released every month at www.thepierian.org. Poetry submissions welcome at our website. Contact info@thepierian.org for all other inquiries.

ISSN 2835-5806

AF407730

Table Of Contents

FOREWORD

The world really does need another poetry magazine, and the proof is in these pages.

The first literary magazine that impacted my worldview was *Granta*. It felt like a lifeline to the literary culture of UK bookstores I had left behind to pursue my doctorate back home in the USA. The stories were cosmopolitan, sharp, emotionally gutting. The covers were stylish.

Granta, like so many other literary magazines, has gone out of business in the two decades since I was a loyal reader. Yet here I am, committed to the endeavor of starting another literary magazine. In large part, that is due to the passions of my editorial partner, the true founder of *The Pierian*, Max Roland Ekstrom.

When I first met Max, he had a couple of poetic endeavors accessible online. One of these was a precursor of today's large language model (LLM) artificial intelligence poetry generators. Max's website would generate ridiculous randomized "poetry" on a variety of topics. As conceptual art, it embodied deep truths about the superficial practice of poetry and criticism at the turn of the century. True humanity wasn't necessary if you spouted the right words.

Max's ambition to found a more lasting journal, however, did persist, and we're coming through on that vision today. Over the course of the last year and ten issues, we published a delightfully varied coalition of writers on our website.

We read completely blind, with each poem served to the editors individually from the submissions database; a fact that has interesting consequences for the ultimate makeup of the journal. If you open most other poetry journals and come across two or three poems by one poet, chances are high that they were submitted together as part of a carefully chosen portfolio. In our case, however, it is most likely that the poems were originally submitted, selected, and published months apart.

Because the poems were not originally selected as portfolios, we have taken the liberty of arranging all the poems in the volume without regard to the common practice of retaining all the poems by one poet together. I'm sure there are or have been other journals and anthologies that operate with this freedom, but it seems unusual enough to merit mention.

Instead of gathering the poems of each poet together, we're striving to let the poems of different authors speak with one another in ways they couldn't do across our brief web issues. Our hope is that as you flip through the magazine and browse for the works of your favorite poets, you will find that their neighbors also have something to offer; a kinship of theme, diction, or insight.

Broadly speaking, we have poems that are enlivened by reference to the texts and traditions of the past: Greek, Roman, Chinese, Babylonian, Hebrew, Welsh, and more. Our Vermont roots also led to the selection of poems that evoke nature and the outdoor life. Poems that experiment with form are scattered throughout the issue.

These various threads seemed to us to come together and complement one another most effectively in one poem, and thanks to the generosity of our *Pierian* subscribers, we have been able to award our 2023 Alexander Pope Award recognizing this poem. Jonathan Ukah's "A Second of Your Life" deploys a fast-flowing, loose pentameter rhythm and Biblical allusions to craft a Pindaric ode in honor, not of a sport, but of simply living a full life.

It has been such an honor to set out on this journey of craft and creation with all of the poets published in the first year of *The Pierian*. We want to make a special acknowledgement of the poets who participated in our online poetry workshop and seminar "The Lyric Self" in the winter of 2022, three of whom are published in this journal: Erica Breen, Bruce Jacobs, and Judith Janoo. Their writing and conversation confirmed us in our belief that the world really does need more small poetry publications, especially if they can contribute to a sense of literary community.

Here's to a joyful and literary 2024!

—Keeley Schell

Jonathan Ukah

A SECOND OF YOUR LIFE

If you give me a second of your life
I could show you how to win a medal,
how to become a champion without a fight,
show you the different fingers of your hand
and how they form the constellations of victory;
though the day has gone into the gloom
you become smaller and smaller each day.
To be reborn is such an easy thing
that we can run naked and still be champions,
if we keep on running when our heart is on fire,
or when we start climbing the hill of age,
your knees failing; your teeth clattering,
your breath coming in like a tree climber's sigh;
or the bush throws its fireballs about;
or the moon suddenly withdraws its light,
throwing you into the deepest darkness.
Be not dismayed when the sky collapses
across your path to weigh you down;
to win a race, you must keep on running,
jumping over hurdles and rocks of old age,
until your body gets used to its lightness
and growing old becomes a closed hole in a wall.
The walls of Jericho fall at the seventh trumpet,
after dreams have accumulated vapours
and the air becomes denser than moisture.

Phil Montenegro

CATHEDRAL

Escuelas Pías de San Fernando, Lavapiés, Madrid

For a moment
the bomb enlarges the cathedral.
Its belltowers rise and burst
as if to proliferate the news of God,
the dome riven like an egg
against a cast-iron sky.

Brick and stone constellate the air.
Confetti of silica and pumice
plumes above terracotta rooftops
and the cathedral collapses inward
upon itself in a gesture of supplication.

A bomb is never allowed choice.
It falls in undiscerning grace
to burn and become anything
it meets, a momentary, ardent
armature of all it destroys.

What took years to build
is undone in an instant
leaving neither the bomb
nor the cathedral, nothing
but a silence mistaken for
the speechlessness of ghosts.

Judith Janoo

FALL SONG

Vivaldi of falling leaves, violin strings,
symphony of all summer has come to—

last juices leaving limbs, drawing in,
leaf crackle of our vinyl 33 needle

note-pressed in grooves of your goodbye.
Birch leaves yellowing into brown curls

like your arms closing around me, maples
out-glowing their green, saying *notice,*

saying *whoop-tee-doo,* saying don't waste
this change, savor what will drop, grant cover

from frost, like sheets we slept between. The beeches
hold on as you did at the end—your showy splendor

measured in shadow, your flare too much to last,
like sunflowers painted by your namesake.

Nothing plain in you, not one cell
gave way without sparks from the bow.

How much you passed on to our children,
tender as leaf veins, coloring the world after you.

I stand listening to the blinding of leaves,
their commanding shiver.

Judith Janoo

INVITATION

Come with me to Pemaquid's shore
late afternoon when the sun's lids
close red and moist
over the weeping ocean
streaking gray sand
leaking as if to harrow
beach peas and peat
wild yarrow's ghostly blossoming
and flax-colored grasses
gone to seed.

Come with me to inlets
where foam feathers
into pools we waited
all our lives to enter,
where winds brush the surface
of what we never said
not dipping into what we wished
or knew how to express,
our children's best becoming
tide pools of unexpected treasure
bright star fish
and flowering purple urchin.

Come with me again
to this teeming shore
where we can leave all
we asked of each other
steeped in these waters
to a briny tea
we drink saying
what we couldn't then
where we can stay
tucked among rocks

like a pair of herring gulls
wading in the waves
that carried
your ashes away

Beth McDonough

UNRELIABLE DIRECTIONS

Another Curling Pond Road sign
enamels directions to a pool
which rarely freezes, and certainly
can't bear weight these days.

Then the related lane a few miles away
leads to no water at all.
Even my local skating pond
is just a junction's sunk remembrance.

Only the air carries the slash dance
of passing blades or the long boom
and brush as some stone hurtles on,
to startle crowds of birds, black

into the tall tops of hacked back
limes and the shake of Corsican pines.
But I only tell you this, form a shape
of stories and news from signs.

Nothing we've seen or heard, only the minds
we try to unknot in storms when we climb
into the net lofts of the cottage we dreamed
we'd always lived in, but never really did.

Paul Jaskunas

CRIMINALS

We paddled out in our kayak
to the center of a lake made gold
by sunset. From the reeds
along the shadowed edge
came a disturbance—ripples,
the soft splash of fins
caught in a torn, tangled,
weed-strewn net

left forgotten by villagers
long ago—two fish,
their amber skins cut
on the string from thrashing
to get into the great water again.

We sliced open the net.

Bleeding from gills and tails,
barely alive, the fish
hung in black water,
yet swollen with life,
eyes and mouths
gaping.

We took them
into the belly of our boat.
On shore, we scraped off
the gold scales, scooped
out the guts, and made
a meal from those fish
caught by treachery,
found by chance.

They cooked up crisp

in the oil, delicious.

When it was all over,
we sat on shore,
stomachs full, and looked
into the dark water
like criminals.

Cela Xie

SALT FOR SODOM

I was fired at one on a Friday afternoon.
What else could I do, in my reverie,
but drive to the beach? I wanted the sea.
I saw a woman half-bared in the tide,
bronze with the last laugh of the light.
I only looked so long against the wind
before the sun left signal flares in my
closed eyes, and I turned for home.
You should pray to be changed by God—
so said my father the night I confessed.
I waited for sand to rise through my hands,
but only the waves came to ruin with me.

Matthew Hutchins

NO LUCK THIS MORNING

Walking with my father, I stumble over his bootprints.
Lever-action clumsy in my arms
like a teenager holding a baby.

He presses the barbed wire of a fence into a V
so I can cross. Lowers his orange mask
to ask, *No luck this morning?*

I do not tell him that I drank two cups
of french pressed coffee against a cedar tree.
Rifle unloaded—out of reach.

I do not speak of the buck that came to me,
movement masked by the rings of fog
it puffed into the air

nor of the minute we spent watching each other
as it stomped damp moss. The rifle forgotten
until it turned back to the tree line.

No luck this morning.

Kim Malinowski

SHOVEL TEST PITS IN WINTER

My shovel beats the earth at 9 a.m.
thermometer still reads 32 degrees

tuft falls away into muddy flowers
ribbon of earth
quakes before me
layer siltier,
less frost

I shed outer layer
beat down the dust
nostrils flaring with sienna
crisp earth turned
thorns buried in palms
price for Munsell,
for stratigraphic wall,
for frost and loam
for the brown on calluses
and brow
for sanctuary

worship sandy tongue
grit and love and time

I strip myself as I journey down,
trowel hits water

suddenly,

I am winter dowsing rod.

Devon Brock

WINTER FUNERARY WITH PRAYER

It took a backhoe to dig below the frostline,
into the clay above the bedrock, for us
to gather on the green welt cleared of snow,
for us, in our hemps and wools to lay
a body down, to return what was
never ours to own—

Our father—

As to the godless, faith briefly.
As to the faithful, black doubt.

Jonathan Ukah

MY MOTHER'S BODY

Sometimes I feel that my mother's body is a country,
with open borders, open doors and windows,
a landscape wider than the width of the sky,
but let it not close like Nigeria, to reason,
good governance, wise decisions and truth.
My mother's body lay in the casket like a letter
written in a moment of deep sadness,
an elegy on the murder of beauty and love,
not yet sealed for fear of losing the spectacle
of her second coming, and second chances;
as a souvenir of tears thudded on the coffin;
my lips scooped up a handful of red sands
from the scab of soil near my mother's grave;
for a long time, it had not rained, and the earth split;
flowers wilted; leaves dried and fell off,
reservoirs of water waited for momentary spitting
to hold down their crumbs from turning violent.
people were already murmuring like Israel at Zin;
I imagine them believing my mother's death
was the reason it had not rained for many days.
Even the sky could no longer wear a makeup
as my mother's body lowered into the smoky hole,
and high notes of mourning slit silence into a frenzy;
amidst the smouldering heat of the evening,
the sky emptied an ocean of water on our compound,
filling every mourning heart with saturation,
falling in sparks of fire, pattering over the roof.
Even in death, mother, you cater for us.

Ghali Greythorne

FAVORED SON

Sow your ash and dust in the scorched husks
of the wheat stalks, broken teeth
collapsing into salt as though God
spilled countries across the fields
and declined to name them. You dance
on idle hands, planting rifles
for headstones—bullets cutting wounds
into the earth as a mosaic of casings and sinew.
Kiss its jaggedness on the forehead
as your favored son then carve into it
an absence of self with knives knapped
from the bones of the once-men
reaching out of the topsoil.

Devon Brock

MANUFACTURE

In its original sense:
to shape with the hands—

how you draw the line
of your lover's jaw
from neck to chin;
how she leans into your palm
as you wipe a tear
from the corner of her eye
with your fingertip.
Remember this

when the clay dries,
when the glaze cracks.

Zachary Daniel

TREASURE

I was a Spanish galleon
and you pitched in my wake
like a heap of crumpled flowers.
It was as though some slow vessel
had dumped the whole meadow of you
over the gunwale
to outpace corsairs.
I trawled my net
around your milkweed shoulders
and hauled you in
by snake-bane and goldenrod,
by columbine and ironwood;
I wanted to claim the very nectar of you.
And how the dumb tongue of my prow
swung over the Mediterranean
toward the reddish sands of Spain,
the waves so still,
as though in awe of our love.
And when we neared the shore
the breakers urged us forward
on white feathers.

D.S. Maolalai

SLIPPING THE TILLER

Like steering a paddleboat
watching for rocks,
I am always in a hurry
but careful of the hull. Today,
going home
on a bike with a bag on my handles,
a bottle of wine
and some biscuits, some bread,
I tried to overtake a pedestrian
by going on grass—lost grip
instead, and slipped sideways—
almost went into him
but dodged
and rolled at traffic
before I stopped.
I choked out my sorries
and he said
it's ok—and why
shouldn't he? He was fine,
hadn't been hurt
and had almost seen
something interesting.
I pushed on, my legs
weak as lace
in old shoes, feeling mud in my tires
and cars charging
like waves, wind in their wake,
slipping and really
quite slippery.

Lilith Morgan Elliott

PORC FAT

Unclean? Perhaps; hopeful of a feast,
to be sure—dressed and garnished
with all this mud exchanged for green.
Oh, to stuff myself with sweets
and be surrounded by pretty things:
the straightened tines of forks,
rows of smiles edge to edge,
framed in champagne flutes;
that all should be so fine in the end,
that there may even be some salivating
over my flesh. What more could I want?
For now, I relish the circle of mud
on my face, and its power over you.
Attend to your flowers, pressed
between lines of Greek and Latin.
You'll soon trade them all for dirt;
and when you join us at the table,
well—I'd rather delight the tongue
than be a starveling mutt underfoot,
unfit even for scraps, nourished
only by the sharp jab of steel-
toed boots. If we're both going to roast,
I'd rather die delicious. Wouldn't you?

Devon Brock

ON A NIGHT LIKE ANY OTHER

Here I am a dolphin, a jellyfish,
a moray eel. I am collateral,
a mercenary reaping as the fisher
stars plunge down their nets,

their baits, the whole
of which draws me up and out,
hand over hand, but wants
nothing of me. My flesh

cannot be sold to the gods
in the marketplace.
I am all bone and envy,
never born to thin air,

but hatched in the murk
of a trawling: wastefish.
Stiff keels cut deep
in this sorrowed gloom,

as what is flung to the deck
is crushed like Cancer, then
kicked through the scupper
for the codmeat of trade.

Adam Haver

ODE TO AMPHITRITE

There is not the Goddess and the Sea,
only a goddess who breathes, and
the waves are her involuntary ways.

She gasps and the tide retreats.
She sighs and the tide returns.
Her heart billows against the rocks.

The surf is Amphitrite, she who encircles,
Goddess who with a golden spindle
weaves the depths and surface of herself,

whose glimmering tunic is a golden palace,
the Nereid queen, the gilded sea, her will
born by chariot, by seahorse hippocamp.

Queen of pearls, whose body forms
the shore, many a sailor has sought in you
delight, only to drown in your embrace.

Zeyu Ma

TO YANG GUIFEI AT MAWEI STATION

Pale blue mists, rising above sorghum fields
carrying marcescence out of valley's umbrage—
no time for homesick glances, carriages grind on
six hundred leagues, from Jiannan to Chang'an
simmering nimbus caterwaul.

Cuckoos cry in harmony with Daoists' cantillation,
my soul has no control of itself, stirring
the skeleton under layers of crimson quilts. I ought
to have renounced imperium at Mawei Station. Too late
I learned to pray before Guanyin's niche, that
begging never wins favors from a Bodhisattva.
"She was treacherous: her death well deserved,"
I deny it in tears—you are faultless,
your fragrance is still unbesmirched.

>   *I dreamt of you dressing*
>   *in a gilded mirror, donning*
>   *your silken-pheasant gossamer,*
>   *rubbing on saffron rouges, waiting*
>   *to hear one soul-snatching incantation.*
>   *If you want (if that brings you home)*
>   *I will promulgate the gods' will, burning*
>   *down my desires, burning down*
>   *every lacquered idol.*

Remember last year's plum rain?
Plumes of smoke engulfed your throat;
amidst chaos you broke free of my grip
disappearing into the whiteness. No remorse—
to the everlasting regret—you surrendered.

I know time dwindles to candle's tears,
so I opened Tongguan's gates, clawing

at seasons' crease. I let the river floods in,
I wanted the apocalypse.

Adam Haver

ENLIL SPEAKS ACROSS THE ALLUVIAL PLAIN

Because they were boisterous and kept
the gods awake, Enlil sent a sudden flood.
Is it enough to tolerate? My vision not
your vision, my leaf on a longer branch,
yours near the canopy, near the furthest
grasp of sun—*quiet now, the waters come.*

He discontinued immortality without
remorse, or a mild remorse unrecorded.
Is your death greater than my death now
that we are mortal? Now that we both bleed
tints of red jealousy, all for the cause of
bold comparisons—*you'll be fine, at first.*

His assembly sent the Bull of Heaven to
slay Gilgamesh after Ishtar was offended.
Who is spurned but those who spurn an ill
attempt at union? Two rivers diverged, the
Tigris swift, the Euphrates enduring, until
confluence—*child, your slumber is my rest.*

Judith Janoo

WHAT CIRCLED US

To my skeptic husband

You say there are no halos,
no glorioles, no coronas at night,
no headdress of tenderness,

no crown molding, hope
for humble ceilings. You say
I only imagine true medicine rings,

these healings, buffalo blood beating
in chests pressed against Earth's skull,
ribs holding an unbroken heart.

Let autumn winds brush
milkweed's silk against your lips,
slipped from its hollowed womb,

let snow kiss your eyelids
as you stand alone,
fingering your ring,

remembering cooking's cumin
scent against my skin,
till beauty begins to ring true.

See the glow of have-nots
we fed under a harvest moon,
each nimbus of streetlights

and headlights, of bright strings
spiraling from eaves—
we had reason for optimism.

J. A. Marcus

THEY SHARED A TRENCH

New York Times, 2/20/23

Within the empty Kropyvnytskyi flat,
a mantel decorated with Christmas lights
lifts the newlyweds' photograph
nestled amid saints' icons.
There the dead soldiers repose, her head
bobbing on the chest of his tunic,
her large eyes tracing a distant cloud
or turbine as her painted nails meet.
Smirking, as if startled from his fall to earth,
he combs his hand through a sea of daisies.

Lilith Morgan Elliott

ONE DAY WE'LL BE ABANDONED

But for now we can clear a space,
collapse all the thresholds between us,
occupy a room both ours and not ours—

sink onto this futon and feel the touches
that linger under the duvet; see light lift
mirages from a mirror when the sun hits

just so, showing all the people who bore
their private longings so close, or thrust them
against the glass, perhaps kissed them there;

touched them, at least, or else left them untouched.
We cannot stay forever. All we leave will fall
in time, through linoleum and limestone;

but we can bare ourselves, and must,
down to the very scrawl of silverfish.
And if our end is only the moving of lips,

we can breathe the dust in and out
of our lungs—pour ourselves over mirrors
and wait for the sun to lift us again;

to be remembered; to be eaten; to become
like the primitive insect, gnawing
all the words we can before we're gone.

Jonathan Ukah

A LITTLE LIFE

I have mastered the art of being wise
and becoming foolish at the same time;
the science of being rich and poor equally.
I have learned to live in the sky
while worshipping the gods of the earth,
where Heaven created the Messiah
whose golden robes sweep the ground
each time He wants the rain to fall.
I am lame and mobile, dumb and talkative;
my silences harvest torrents of noise
that cause tremors to seize the seas;
some days I'm alive and dead to the bones,
a body and a spirit, hovering in a tunnel
where darkness dwells and light will come,
a man sitting on the tripod of fate;
walking the lanes of pain, reaching the top,
when happiness lies at the top and bottom.
I have known the thrills of going downhill,
and wandering uphill is like a fulfilment,
while it's still a struggle trying to know
the difference between what I say and get.
Grandeur and grace, humility and shame
battle for control of my body, to achieve
the selfish and selfless goals I cast in stone;
if I am lucky to escape the clutch of evil
God will possess me and reign forever.
Only then can I confirm, with life and death,
that I always believe when I'm downhill,
that there will be power in my gagged tongue
when I declare I have reached my goals in life,
or that this little life is a thing worth doing;
never a contradiction but a completion,
an immortal requiem for a perfect life.

Erica Breen

CUSSED

My son took me to visit
a warehouse for old people.
He says I need to get ready
to be packed away.

Their hair is neatly combed.
Pastel sweaters clean
like one of those store-bought
Easter baskets
smothered in cellophane.

They all smile, they all
use their walkers like obedient
lame dogs.

They fill their rooms with clutter
to hide
their feelings.

They have given up,
you can see it in the way
they stoop.
You can smell it, stale warmed-over
canned green beans.

I wore my red shirt.
I left my walker
in the car.
My son says I have to get ready,
the packers are coming,
my son says I should sell
my piano.

I told them my memory is
pretty good.

I don't look like an old lady.
I left my walker in the car,
I held the railing,
I asked if I come here,
can I have my car back?

I would drive to the grocery store,
to the church bazaar.
I would drive to the doughnut shop.
I would drive to the mountains.

I would escape from the basket
with my red shirt
like a flag.

I would speed,
the wind mussing my hair.

Mark J. Mitchell

ENTRY RONDO À LA HOTEL KRUPA

No drums allowed, a sign reads. The street door
opens on white and scuffed black tiles. A floor
piano and guest get lost in ghost tunes
left in Hotel Krupa. Voices might croon
old Crosby songs. No one calls out for more.

The entrance clicks closed. You've lived here before.
You'll be back. Gold-toned boxes waiting for
mail behind broken locks. Check out time's noon.
No drums

allowed. Hotel Krupa keeps time—two fours
to the bar. Six or nine beats. Rhythm's lore
runs wild in this foyer, covering wounds
old players wear. It should get torn down soon
but won't fall. Not many rules, but one more
sign: No drums.

Ian McGrath-Santowski

AFTER THE STREET LIGHTS TURNED ON

A man sings for a woman
below the magnolia tree,
blooming, but not
yet fully bloomed,

as pink petals,
soft as skin,
lay one
beside the other
on the bed
of the aging bench.

The woman sings along,
under her breath,
so as not to disturb
the lingering sound
of a strumming guitar.

Philip Dunkerley

SUNDAY MORNING

Who put that haunting *andante cantabile* refrain into my head
where it stays and plays again and again? And who wrote
the poem that takes me off to *Minas de Mazarrón*, and an old
fundición in Spain?

Breakfast of dried apricots, the colors of autumnal gold.
The dark coffee beans, the smell and the touch of Brazil.
A book—*The Art of Growing Old*—waiting for me still.
A black stone, obsidian. A buzzard's feather found in a field.
A sequoia cone.

I'm pottering, distracted by rhyme, fingers pattering away.
What's the time? Nearly eight. I got things to do today.
They can wait.

Devon Brock

INHERITANCE

To do poor well,
take down granny's
black skillet, its mettle
keen with decades
of scrapple and cheek.

Take its heft in your wrist.
Mix fistfuls of onion
and greens with salt
and wilt them as the iron
ticks with heat. Then,

take cornmeal and eggs,
milk and oil and whisk.
Whisk until your batter
is smooth and your will
is as sturdy as johnnycake.

Ella Rous

GHAZAL AT DAWN

I had to watch your face to see the light coming.
A mirror for a horizon that was behind me, a sight coming

to touch my mind gently and lift off, a butterfly, delicate, fragile
and transitory. I blinked and the beauty ebbed, the white coming

over the horizon, so cold and clean as to purify and excruciate.
The final wash of terror over our bodies. This isn't Christ's coming:

the blood in the water, the acid in the rain, the settling of locusts
over a field. Only, I am the blood, the acid, the locusts. It's a blight coming.

But I'll wait for something to harm or wrong, and for something
to harm or wrong you. In the meantime, I watch the mites coming

and whorling in the strands of sunlight. I avoid your touch
and I dream of blades in the dark. You are the right coming,

and I am the wrong coming, and I want to avenge you. It is all
I know how to do for you. And still I fear the night coming.

Call me what you will: glint, molar, luster, baby's breath,
honey, darling. Ellie, E.J., Ella. I won't see the light coming.

Robin Alexander

SITTING ON A TRAIN AS IT HITS SOMEONE

At first, it's an inconvenience:
turbulence in the back teeth,
steel screaming for the mile

it takes to stop.
You ride a stampede
of bison—dark shapes,

churning dust. A pounding of earth
you can bite down on. The rattle
of stones. The shudder of an engine

killed, only noticed when it's gone,
hot stillness settled in place.
A wasp draws yellow circles

round the back
of a girl's head.
A spectacle case snaps shut.

You pretend to read
for the next hour,
'til the engine limps

to the nearest station,
beaten. You look at the ripple
spreading over the field outside,

the pale underbellies
of grass blades.
That distant, humming sea

of cricket legs. Up close,
the throat's pulse—the strange guilt
of the heartbeat, the breath.

Zachary Daniel

THE RED HEART'S TILT

For Rimbaud

Through bristles and fern fronds, flailing ground
the red heart, wheeling, slant in sun
and plaited grass, makes its mad dash
for the violet-patch, for distant honeydew.

And didn't you, red heart, ride
the blanched waves, rebuff the wind,
send the soot hooting from your vents,
couch your lance, tense your veins?

Reins, red heart, *reins*—too quickly
and you'll reach the fence, visor
battered, gleaming pauldrons rent—
what trumpets would herald you then?

What decibel wrung from the temples?
What silk garment thrown over
your oxen shoulder; what crocus
pinned to your luminous breast?

Red heart, the chase is never finished,
nothing pitied there in your quest across
the gumplants, the violent sprouting land.
The blood will fill your boots like wineskins.

A river stirs far beneath the ground;
A prong, an angry word is on your tongue—
speak it now before the daylight's gone.
Others will begin where I've succumbed!

Paul Jaskunas

CLOUDS LIKE MUSCLES

Looking up the famous Auden poem
Where the dogs go on with their doggy life,
I notice on the inside cover
the words

clouds like muscles

penned in faint ink
by my hand long ago.

I was in London then, new to Auden,
to Hampstead Heath and beer
and the weight of one-pound
coins in my pocket. *Clouds
like muscles* perhaps I wrote
in Hyde Park or Vauxhall
or aboard a bus, while gawking
at a patch of ribboned sky.

I remember nothing of the sight,
or of that day, the tea
I might have sipped,
the streets I might have braved.
That hour, those rippling clouds,
that suffering boy with his paperback poems—

I wander back to him now
and sit beside him in the grass
along the Serpentine.

He knows nothing of all he will do.

I stay with him awhile
and let him confess his loneliness.
I remind him of what he will soon forget:

that even the ship in Auden's poem,
that saw Icarus fall to the sea,
Had somewhere to get to and sailed calmly on.

I tell him to remember his sorrow is small
and the sky above vast and strong.

Zeyu Ma

HITHER TO SILK-WASHING STREAM

"What are we to this Amsterdam?
Not your Leica photos, or Instagram.

You know the museums by heart, you
have gone off to parties in Overtoom,"

I asked while leaning on your shoulder,
sailing downtown along Prinsengracht.

We expended our youth, our 21, from
one canal to another, splitting ripples,

drifting between continents, spilling life
into secret missions, in one long exile.

"Everywhere, counting the roads not taken
is difficult, however far we escaped home.

Amsterdam is just another city, it has blue arteries;
wherever we can sail, wherever is home." Yes,

parting with motherland was a dangerous affair:
remember our farewell? Last July when that

putrid-green heat stroked your heart, we soared
above the stratosphere, back to your Yangtze town.

Sailing under Jiajing-era caverns, through dense
lotus blooms, drowning in its calcium scent.

En route to our elementary school
startled herons flew, south and north.

Kim Malinowski

KIM AND IKEA PUT TOGETHER HER BOOK

Take down that cracked leather volume,
dusty and timeless, unwrap with box cutter.
Inventory the pieces. Each word must
enjamb correctly, each screw must hold.
Dactyls unfurl like reminiscing scrolls.
Place the verbs and nouns together with each
screw and washer labeled C and E.

Do not forget to inspect edges—the pages must line up,
or it will be unstable. No one wants a labyrinth
of metaphor to topple onto their toe.

Now, gather the wooden pegs and the articles.
Gently use a mallet to hammer pesky words out of lexicon.
Keep strange 19th-century euphemisms—
they must be hammered in, rusty nail or no.

Rotate. Observe each edge—
press into water-damaged antiquity.
Tales and Allen wrenches crack tongue,
blood trickles as edge slices thumb, should've sanded
that particular participle down more.
Plyers and bloodshed are offerings to literature.
The gods like Post-it notes and pens,
but prefer MacGyver-like instincts—if a book needs
a new cover, then damn it, use a paperclip and some floss.
Gum is for amateurs.

Make love to dust and binding.
(The directions say not to take this direction "literally.")
I do not keep the cover I tore in gleeful abandon,
only torn manuscripts
to mend—word quilts
to cover my reverie.

I place the Allen wrench in cramped tool drawer.
I reason the book will not fall apart.
There are two extra screws, one washer, a nail.
Those pieces must have been extra,
like the articles I took the mallet to.

Stephen Kingsnorth

ROAD BUMPS

My poem tends to pidgin style,
in English lingo, but curtailed,
for as compacting wordy terms,
it's apt for gaps. When definite,
assume the reader telegrams,
inserts the tetragrammaton,
the word unspoken, but known there,
a gap in line, but owned by them,
or to be frank, the article.
As in France, wanting bread, I said
une pain s'il vous plait; she made plain,
with quiver lip, this tourist pain,
un *pain*, as if a crime, but knew,
and took my cash, baguette in hand.

So play along and act your part,
as hear the poser, apron tied,
and give reply, whatever tide.
Why should the stage work entertain,
without response from that fourth wall—
for readership, a talking point,
who adds what's missing, as reviews.
Some haiku with a broader brush,
potholes meant to slow your drive,
road bumps to frustrate the rush,
and workmen from a stripy tent
who dig, survey, stop work for tea—
the choice is yours, no foreman here—
keep digging, drinking, or clock off.

Donald Goodbrand Saunders

GILGAMESH IN SIDURI'S

Siduri the barmaid-goddess, veiled woman of the vine, of the wine-vats beside the sea...

Same again love not from around here are you I never forget a face comes with the job see you raid or trade no quest then we get a lot of that in here I tell them look you're wasting your time east west home's best wife and kiddies but will they listen each to his own though I say JUST WAIT YOUR TURN commercial traveller then oh king that's nice don't talk much do you I like that in a man you got a name then I'VE ONLY ONE PAIR OF HANDS Gil- Gilga- whatever I knew you weren't from these parts we'd one in yesterday weird old bugger pardon my French and who might you be I sez Utnapishtim he sez Ut-na-pish-tim well I nearly wet meself but I didn't say nothing 'cos it's a customer see and I'M COMING HOLD YOUR HORSES give me strength so he starts on about the floods where he is like it's the end of the world I mean everyone's on about the weather these days call yourselves sea peoples I ask you and anyway why worry life's too short darling and he gives me this funny look and I kid you not nearly a smile and he says he's got to catch the ferry and he's off that's right the Dilmun ferry yes it's leaving in about let me see ten no five minutes oh and goodbye to you too now that was just rude not my day is it RIGHT. WHO'S NEXT?

Zachary Daniel

SLUG AT SIX

I found him in the garden taking shelter
under the cool shade of a shovel blade
that I'd turned over, intent on digging up
the gold I knew some pirate buried after
clambering the slick banks of the Ohio.

His palpitating eyes, his sheen of oil
glistened just as well to soothe my greed.
His leopard spots were like a creature's
camouflage shorn from some local jungle.
I caught him unaware, pounding flat

into the soil, then cut him clean in half
hefting the spade's narrow bevel.
For the corpse I dug a shallow grave
and held a ceremony with some beetles
who swung their black heads in sorrow,
fretting to and fro like Aunt Pauletta.

My mother found me at the site of mourning,
saw my sag from the big bay window,
and I cried wet lumps into her shoulder
but wouldn't tell her what I had done.

Lilith Morgan Elliott

WRITE SOMETHING NICE, LOVE

the cat, say, claws retracted
over the lip when he settles,
fangs overlarge when he yawns.

Write something warm—
how sunlight filters through
chlorophyll and wriggles
through the windowscreen
to fertilize the pages
of the book you hold—
how the words turn over
in mounds and bloom
behind your eyelids.

And isn't this summer?
Does it have to be anything
more than the grass
without its scratching, the heat
without its cancers, the pools
without their drownings?
Can't you write about summer
without it ever ending?

J. A. Marcus

STREET FIGHTERS

For K.K.

The six-button Street Fighter case
we used to mash at the town pizza spot,
the crimson seating, and its graying boss—

retired, evicted, razed. Before all shut
down, and before the final bout where Ken
and Ryu's flame froze within 16-bit

unscrolling vistas of maritime moon-
lit docks and paper lamps, we trained to store
their brilliant searing blue and red dragon

attacks as our reflex. In August's air
we broke for college without looking back,
leaving those rivals to a repertoire

that now I yearn to save from fading into black.
What of our teenage glory days? What hell
it was to be a nobody, no luck

with bad girls, fast cars, rock bands, or baseball—
never any quarter but plenty dime,
always a step short on the hero's trail,

lacking dad's praise, cursed with idle time;
no kingdom's quest awaited us as men
but the loss of dancing within a game.

Adam Todd

ALDRICH AMES

Just write it in chalk on a blue mailbox
Spell out your sins, name your price then
name some names, and if you're drunk enough
while you're at it tell your wife about the girls in Mexico.

Don't put it off, Rick.
Don't let your boss know, Rick.
Don't leave the files on the subway, Rick.

You say we're making a huge mistake and
we have the wrong man, but

your new wife's on the phone to Colombia;
we're listening to her talk. Dan's on the headset,
Diane's jotting it word-for-word, Jeanne's rifled around
your trash and Sandy's started the paperwork and my lord, Rick,
      there's a lot.

It'll be adios to the Jag;
the house'll get sold. Play ball and maybe
life sans parole in a Terre Haute or a Florence High.

Have a drink, Rick, and let us know.
Have a drink and let us know.

Ghali Greythorne

I Am Not God, but I Am Sorry

Clamp a misgiving to your chest. Let it dismantle your focus
as I take the pen and double-tap the signature line. Attune

to dissonance—cresting amplitudes as thoughts riot
like weaponized tuning forks: stropped and honed

until able to sever angels' wings, hiding their faces
from heaven. Words slither through us like polonium

from teabags, principles as bullets fed through the chamber.
Remember that integrity is a property of objects and nations

permit conscience to twinkle about the edge of a bayonet,
splitting moments into forgone conclusions. Walk away. I cannot

make whole haphazard shards when every joining shatters
elsewhere; rearranging our fissures until we are ghosts

hoping what flickered within
finds us worthy of stillness.

Mark J. Mitchell

WITNESS PROTECTION

Around the time her mirror snapped, she wrote
names of lapsed gods—their long, dangerous names—
on hems of drapes. Her talisman—her hope
against plague and fire. She let her pets out.
Then she shuffled old cards, spread a long game

around time. Her compact snapped. So she wrote
small verbs on her palm. She stumbled through days
like that—half-dressed in darkness, left without
her face for comfort. She waited for blame
to wash over with its red tide. Small doubts

about time made her mirror snap. She wrote
on shards, with long fingers, all those false names
they asked to hear before they'd let her out.

Adam Haver

THE SOWER AREPO HOLDS WITH EFFORT THE WHEELS

Each spring the fallow fields await the sower
like a savior come to give them purpose,
divine if not destined, the mounded rows.

Arepo has taxied the fields for so long he knows
no other route to take, from seed to harvest
he holds the wheel straight until winter's signs.

The seedlings know the land before they grow,
their parents having instilled a legacy of what
they know of this soil, blessed by Arepo's hand.

And when the sower's bones mingle with the seeds,
he'll find a sweet familiarity within the ground,
as all the fields rejoice at his rooted homecoming.

Phil Montenegro

MILAGRO

Madrid, 2015

As if accident could not be
necessary

as it was to San Isidro,
saint of this dry city,

who struck his plow deep
into the parched ground

only to dowse a spring
like a held breath

broken

and wash the sick
free of disease

with the water
he'd ruptured open.

Today, I woke to a river
where a street had been.

An uprage of water
on the run,

it ran

slashing over brick and tar
in its tameless

timeless
    spate

through the spokes of a bike
and the legs of a dog

to slake the streets
it had run beneath,

and the firemen
bearing picks and shovels

on their shoulders
saw only an attack

on their well-seamed order,
running frantic

to seal a fractured pipe
and relieve their panic,

taking what mystery
rose to flood the street

for granted

as if saints were only men
granting blessings no one wanted.

Bruce Jacobs

SECOND CHANCES

In a two a.m. reverie
I scale the vertical sisal climbing rope
on my first attempt
much to the dismay of my Phys. Ed. teacher

I discover my childhood
Lionel train set
So that's where you stored it
Grandpa

In slumbrous research within the field-stone-walled
Lawrence Park Library, amidst
encyclopediae, microfiche and Dewey Decimals
I re-establish my universe of elocution

Chauffeuring Booker T. Jones
we meet up with Keith Emerson
at the Hammond Organ factory
none of us happy with modern techno

I dance a Welsh *Nantgarw*
with Morgan le Fay in King Arthur's Court
a *fata morgana*; heel-to-toe
twirling in a complex mirage

Licking my fingertips
I masterfully bake a
rhubarb *gateau renverse*
upside down like an inverted childhood

I beseech a Chilean black widow *por favor*
Can you please have a sudden inclination

and choose the hapless *cucaracha*
instead of my big toe

It feels good to be granted a second chance

Simon Christiansen

THE LIGHT OF WEIGHTS AND MEASURES

The metre was the length
of a bar
in a vault
in France.

Had it been stolen,
would the world have become indefinite?
Would the thieves have traversed
an unspeakable distance
to escape with their loot?

Would we have walked forever,
attempting to find our homes,
listening to the sirens,
searching for what was lost?

Would they have tried
to return the stolen beam
of knowledge, only to find
themselves lost in the
twilight of topology?

They could have unwrapped
the rod, raised it above
their heads, to guide
the way; a magic wand
dispelling the fog.

Afraid of being caught,
they kept it hidden.

Max Roland Ekstrom

ION'S PROFESSION

Ezra Pound, Sylvia Plath, Robert Lowell, Bob Kaufman: for these twentieth-century poets, the border between creativity and madness was porous. Many other twentieth-century lights, though less notorious, belong in this family of troubled minds. Theodore Roethke, John Berryman, Randall Jarrell, Anne Sexton, David Schubert, Hayden Carruth, Allen Ginsberg and any number of others did not approach any reasonable standard of mental health. Yet none of these accomplished, complex, and fascinating personalities can be reduced to a label. No poet wants their work and legacy to be explained away by illness.

But when we hear of a poet living a life that fits within social norms, we are prone to suspicion. Shouldn't it take exclusion or suffering—more than mere eccentricity—to become a real poet? Many of our finest living poets are open about their struggles. Natasha Trethewey speaks of trauma; Louise Glück, anorexia; Ocean Vuong, substance abuse. Not that it surprises us. We prefer our heroes well-seasoned, and celebrity culture has conditioned us to take our schadenfreude where we can get it.

It is no surprise that fame gets quite dark quite fast. The life of Byron demonstrates that. The surprise is that it seems no different at all levels of success. Most of the dedicated, aspiring poets I've had the pleasure of working with are struggling with *something*, often something pretty heavy. Does the discipline attract practitioners who want to assuage the loneliness of an outsider mentality, or does the practice of poetry itself lead its aficionados to psychological challenges?

Olympic swimmer Michael Phelps discovered that his size-14 feet, however ungainly on land, conveyed a distinct advantage when submerged. Likewise, a prospective poet may consider their own social dysfunction a feature, not a bug. The story of madness and inspiration is a story as old as philosophy—Plato captures the gist of it in his dialogue *Ion*, in which the eponymous rhapsode is interrogated by Socrates about the nature of his verse-mania.

Poetry can benefit from mental abnormality while also soothing it. While these two psychological positions on poetry seem to be in logical contradiction, the aspiring poet feels a growing certainty that in poetry, as in aquatics, the strictures of dry land need not apply. What loftier purpose could an art form serve than to release psychic pain? The shop-talk of poets seems to bear out their psychological specialty. They speak of catharsis, of persona, of symbolism, association, and myth. Poets, more than any other artists, seem to embrace the terminology of psychology as their own.

Under this rubric, the development of 20th-century literature follows a clear progression, like the current of a river. The dam break of Freudian thought influences Modernism, generating a movement intent on breaking taboos on topic and style while shedding traditional poetic forms. Exponents like Eliot, Pound, H.D., Williams, and Moore reposition poetry away from its moribund Christian superstition, diving into the deep end of the psycho-sexual.

This watershed release of the unconscious carries us naturally through the Beats—Ginsberg, Ferlinghetti—to the confessional poetry of Bishop, Lowell, and Roethke, and on to the end of the twentieth century with Kunitz and Graham. The centrality of psychology remains intact today. As the aperture of poetry opens to a greater diversity of voices and backgrounds, the bedrock marriage of poetry and psychology seems secure.

Yet a view of poetic excellence as a continuum that dawned with Freud and has progressed steadily to a deeper understanding of the human psyche is myopic. If you've read a book printed before Goethe, you know that psychological sophistication was not invented by Modernism; subjectivity and depth are core features of literature of all times and cultures.

The idea that the criticism of poetry, or its practice, is reducible to a subdomain of psychology was already thoroughly refuted by Lionel Trilling more than seventy years ago in essays collected in his book *The Liberal Imagination*. Trilling is respectful of Freud, whose death and impact were still being processed by Trilling's New York intellectual circle, but his careful evaluation of Freud's writing demonstrates why we should "accept neither Freud's conception of the place of art in life nor his application of the analytic method." To paraphrase Trilling, neurosis cannot explain why a writer is great any more than it can explain why a businessperson is successful. It can be part of an explanation, but not the only part.

Fortunately, many aspiring poets who at first approach the field with a narrow psychological orientation continue to study and read more broadly and deeply. This path leads to intellectual nourishment, even if the taste for psychoanalysis never totally subsides. For example, re-reading Freud with a firmer classical basis makes his work more lively and sympathetic, and his universe of Greek borrowings that have entered our parlance feel vital again—narcissism, psyche, ego, oedipal, hysterics, catharsis, eros, and so on. As Freud wrote in a letter to his colleague Jung, "We must be careful when besieging Troy."

Freud's great contribution to our culture is not that authors' books, like patients' minds, can be analyzed using his clinical methodology. It is the exact opposite. His era had just begun to formalize literary studies as a rigorous method of textual analysis. Freud realized the mind could be treated in exactly the same way—as a text to be studied more or less dispassionately.

§

As I continue to discuss the role of psychology in contemporary poetry, it is imperative that I differentiate carefully between production and reception—what a poet consumes from their milieu in order to create a poem, versus what intellectual approach readers could benefit from in order to appreciate it.

Poetry is often produced under a fog of mystification and misdirection. That opium is connected to Coleridge's poetic production does not mean his readers must study pharmacology. Yeats took his ouija board very seriously and dabbled in fencing, just as Denise Levertov was a dedicated student of yoga. This does not make these pursuits prerequisite to understanding their work. Hobbies and vices that stimulate a poet's imagination (or that they *claim* stimulate them) change with the times, for fashion is a fundamental component of aesthetics. Psychology informs many twentieth- and twenty-first-century poets, but it is not the most essential context for the understanding of their art.

Production and reception are common to the larger family of fine and performing arts. The most laser-focused aspiring dancer, too busy in the studio for the idleness of the classroom, still invariably develops a practical knowledge of the reception of their art form. Upon joining a company, they will absorb the repertoire, travel, perform, and most importantly, socialize. They will internalize a sense of precedent and perspective, guided as much by nuggets of lore regarding Nijinski or Balanchine as by anything more formal. In this manner, they become competent at the reception of their art form, not just the practice of it.

The poet, whose trade both necessitates and nurtures a greater degree of isolation, cannot expect any comparable on-the-job training in poetic reception, and a few hours of workshop per week pales in comparison to the dancer's exhausting regimen. The dancer's daily grind is based, down to its finest minutiae, on imitating the positions of those with more experience. Just as gravity refines, through resistance, the dancer's physique, the pressure of precedent opposes, and thus strengthens, the dancer's artistic sensibility. As skill and confidence grow in the mirror of precedent, the dancer's pride of pedagogical lineage is as natural as it is unavoidable. Each dancer tailors, adjusts, and reimagines, but mimicry forms the cornerstone of learning.

Novice poets are subject to no such strictures from their mentors, at least not today. Previous generations cut their teeth on Roman, Edwardian, and Romantic verse forms from a young age. Today's aspiring writers ejaculate, "but I don't want to write like anybody else!" Fortunately, mimicry is not the only school of imitation, and a softer diffusion of forms, temperaments, topics, and fashions can be absorbed by simply reading widely. Assuming the poet has a standing invitation from their librarian, and a genuine curiosity in their chosen discipline, a little diligence is all of what is required to awaken what Trilling called "a sense of the past".

Poems always evoke the themes, sounds, and imagery of poems before them, both directly and indirectly; it's not possible to discern accident from intention infallibly. The skilled poet is free to play this ambiguity to advantage. Harold Bloom, in "The Art of Reading Poetry," gives the example of the word "ruins." He writes that this word, whenever it appears in a poem, has a "figurative power…[that] seems endless," because every poet confronts the discarded materials of language that once constituted the castle of their forebears.

The art of poetry has a relationship to its tradition that is intertwined with its practice in ways that ultimately defy easy comparison to any other art. Poets make stuff out of words, and these words are freighted by previous coinage. While superficially similar to the psychological notion of association, literary allusion is a technique that must be studied and developed, irrespective of the poet's own personality and tendencies.

Returning to our distinction above between production and reception, we can now observe that in order to produce a successful poem, the poet must be aware of reception and undaunted by the futility of trying one's hand against prior greats. The reader must be convinced, or the very least, made to blink first. Like Prospero's island, the satisfactions of a poem are fabrications, "such stuff as dreams are made on." Elements of biography and psychology may be recruited to work their magic, but first and foremost it's the sound, shape, and rhythm that hold the spell.

A sense of the past is one of many senses that may delight readers. Others include a sense of place, of presence, of contemporaneity, of dream, of clarity, and of conviction itself. These emergent properties of a poem are all fabrications. As readers, we cannot discern with any certainty whether these effects required decades of preparation or just good lighting. We can't know what's hard-won or cheaply staged, and attempts at speculation rarely end well, as this famous anecdote illustrates:

Frank O'Hara introduced his occasional poem "Lana Turner has collapsed!" at a poetry reading in 1962, explaining to the audience that he had written the poem on the Staten Island ferry en route to the reading. Robert Lowell was also in attendance that day, and when it came time for him to read, Lowell apologized for not having written his poem on the spot too.

Today we live in a period where attitudes toward the past, and particularly the value of studying and preserving it, are shifting rapidly. We are less curious about it; we condescend to thinkers and artists of earlier eras and the scent of their prejudices repulses us, like the suitor of Jonathan Swift's "The Lady's Dressing Room" bolting at the sight of his beloved's chamber-pot.

§

Psychology cannot make a science of poetry, nor does it offer a shortcut to poetic excellence. Yet however much we may wish to lift our field off the analyst's couch, we should not be too hasty.

I have been part of a moderating team for a poetry forum on Reddit for several years, and a constant throughout has been a high volume of suicide poems. Many of the poems read like crude notes taped to the proverbial closet door, while others attempt excited imagery around suicidal ideation.

I have no idea whether posting these poems helps or hurts their authors' odds of survival. Yet despite our efforts as moderators to respond with suicide prevention information and immediate, timely resources for those in crisis, the poems nevertheless attract vast virtual crowds of one-click samaritans. The comment sections are piled deep with formulaic bromides like "it gets better bro" that wholly ignore the text of the poem and opt instead to respond to its author.

These texts, bypassing the usual defenses of audiences, activate the desire of the reader to rid themselves of guilt. By fishing for pity, suicide notes multiply like weeds through concrete, filling the cracks and forming a kind of permanent background radiation.

Poems that touch on themes of suicide, self-harm and mental illness were also common during my time advising and coaching poets. I always begin any discussion of such work with the caveat that sharing poems with me is no substitute for getting treatment from a professional of an entirely different stripe. Poetry and psychology must recognize that they are distinct disciplines with distinct values and deeply different aims and areas of expertise.

Data speak to the depth of the problem. A 2013 study examined the records of nearly 1.2 million Swedish subjects and concluded that "being an author was specifically associated with increased likelihood" of many serious mental disorders, as well as "substance abuse" and "suicide" (Kyaga et al.).

Let us return to what Plato said of Ion's madness. Ion was out of his mind because it was required during his work as a rhapsode performing and interpreting poetry for a live audience. At other times, he was as calm and collected as Socrates himself; his condition was not persistent. When Trilling examines Freud's ideas of neurosis in literature, he rejects the idea that amplitude of neurosis should correspond with amplitude of artistic significance. In art, neuroses, large and small, "must be understood as exemplifying cultural forces of great moment," lest they be "meaningless or merely personal." Trilling, diverging from Plato, embraces the psychological truth that literary culture is created by the transmutation of inner disturbance into lasting beauty, but he rejects psychology's tendency to conflate the two.

Beauty and truth are lofty goals, and most of us, even our most celebrated and talented, usually fall short of Keats' standard. Objectively, there is no rational reason for any of us to keep on trucking in the face of eternal futility—as Bob Dylan quipped, "The world don't need any more poems, it's got Shakespeare." Despite our spells of wishful thinking, we working poets mostly understand this. We know poetry is not going to solve life's serious problems. We also know, from lived experience, that it comes at a cost of time, treasure, and even mental wellness. Sure, we wouldn't mind a little praise, but that's not why keep at it. We do it as a service to the art form that we love.

Every poem is a marriage of waking and dreaming, of clarity and obscurity. Every poet ties themself to the mast, daring madness. The temptation, as ever, is not to tighten the knots, but cut the rope.

Works Cited

Bloom, Harold. "The Art of Reading Poetry." *The Best Poems of the English Language: From Chaucer Through Robert Frost.* Harper Perennial, 2004, pp. 1-29.

Freud, Sigmund, and C. G. Jung. *The Freud/Jung letters : The Correspondence Between Sigmund Freud and C.G. Jung.* Edited by William McGuire, translated by Ralph Manheim and R. F. C. Hull, Princeton University Press, 1974.

Hartman, Anne. "Confessional Counterpublics in Frank O'Hara and Allen Ginsberg." *Journal of Modern Literature*, vol. 28, no. 4, 2005, pp. 40-56. Project MUSE, doi.org/10.2979/jml.2005.28.4.40.

Kyaga, Simon et al. "Mental Illness, Suicide and Creativity: 40-year Prospective Total Population Study." *Journal of Psychiatric Research*, vol. 47, no. 1, 2013, pp. 83-90. doi.org/10.1016/j.jpsychires.2012.09.010.

Trilling, Lionel. "Art and Neurosis." *The Liberal Imagination.* New York Review Books, 2008, pp. 160-80.

Trilling, Lionel. "Freud and Literature." *The Liberal Imagination.* New York Review Books, 2008, pp. 34-57.

Zollo, Paul. "Bob Dylan: The Song Talk Interview." *Bread Crumb Sins*, www.interferenza.net/bcs/interw/1991zollo.htm. Transcription of 1991 interview from Genuine Bootleg Series #3 booklet.

The Pierian is only possible with the financial support of poets, readers, and friends. If you wish to join them in supporting our mission, please visit www.patreon.com/thepierian for more information, or use the QR code below.

9 798868 929571